Words to know

spring or
fall clothes

raincoat

hat

rubber
boots

jacket

summer
clothes

winter
clothes

3

I wear these clothes in **winter**.

glove

scarf

hat

mitten

winter
coat

snow
pants

sweater

boots

These clothes keep me warm when it is cold.
They keep me dry in the snow.

I wear these clothes in **spring** and **fall**. They keep me dry when it rains. They keep me warm.

hood

hat

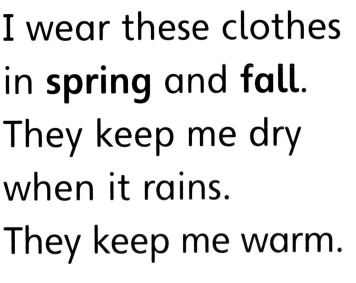

raincoat

jacket

rubber boots

It is cool in the spring and fall.
I wear a jacket and a hat.

I wear these clothes in **summer**.
They keep me cool when it is hot.

sunhat

sunglasses

dress

tee shirt

shorts

sandals   running shoes

In summer, we like to swim.
We wear our **bathing suits**
when we swim.

I wear a **bathrobe** after my bath.
It feels warm and soft.

I wear **pajamas** when I go to bed.
My pajamas have stars on them.

My friends and I
like to wear bright colors.

Name all the colors we are wearing.
Which color do you like the best?

What are these special clothes?

When do children wear them?

Helping others

The clothes I wear helps children become aware of the importance of dressing for different seasons and kinds of weather. Unfortunately, some children do not have clothing to keep them warm or cool throughout the year. Encourage students to think of others and donate any extra clothing, boots, and shoes to a local charity. In winter, children could also donate mittens or hats to give to people in need.

Dress for the seasons

A fun activity to reinforce the different kinds of clothes is to cut out pictures from catalogs or draw images of different seasonal clothing items, such as a winter coat, scarf, mittens, sandals, bathing suit, or sun hat. Draw four outlines of bodies on large pieces of paper—one for each season. Invite the children to "dress" the figures for the different seasons. Children can sort through the pictures and determine which articles of clothing are appropriate for different seasons and types of weather. What other items might they need to protect their bodies, such as sunglasses, sunscreen, or umbrellas? To reinforce clothing vocabulary, you can write clothing words on cards and use the words, instead of pictures, to dress the figures.

Special clothes

Ask the children to look at the clothing on pages 14–15. When do people wear special types of clothes such as uniforms, costumes, and cultural dress?